The Doctor Series

Sean Flaherty

PRINTED IN THE UNITED STATES

TEXT SET IN GARAMOND

ISBN: 978-0-692-88385-3

LIBRARY OF CONGRESS CONTROL NUMBER: 2017941276

PUBLISHED BY CECILIA FLAHERTY

Introduction to The Doctor Series

The Doctor Series is a collection of poems written by Sean Michael Flaherty from the 9th of May to the 17th of December 2014, just two weeks before his death. They tell the story of Sean Flaherty's last stand, from his diagnosis of stage four colon cancer to his final recognition that he would not survive this fight. These poems are painfully brilliant in their illumination of his inner and outer struggles during the most important bout of his life, which he lost on January 4, 2015.

Sean gave up trying to get published in the traditional sense many years ago, but he never stopped writing. He saw publication as a distraction from the work itself, and tied too much to the whims of fate. He once told me he'd finally be published when he was dead. I stupidly responded that I looked forward to writing the introduction. Fuck us both.

In providing you an introduction to this collection, then, let me start by saying that despite its subject matter, this is not a book about cancer. Cancer is just the name of the demon that finally took Sean down, for Sean was always looking over his shoulder, Death trailing behind him, mocking from the shadows; Sean was haunted by specters, demons, horror movie monsters, and comic book super villains, all coming to steal his life, take away his happiness, tear apart his love, and leave him bloody and wanting on the ground.

Sean's writing had always dealt with death, disappointment, betrayal, loss, and love. Nothing and no one, including himself, was out of bounds of his acid wit as he explored these themes as a poet. He believed that the world was full of monsters, and his work reflected that, but he also saw a great goodness rising up from the struggle against the darkness, and his work and his life reflected that too. This collection, then, is really the last battle of a life-long war waged against the dark, where Sean finally engages Death, mano a mano.

Sean developed his own idiosyncrasies with his writing while at Bennington College in the mid-1980s, where we were both students together and became fast friends. From the very earliest of his work I read, Sean chose 12 point Antigua, then later 14 point Garamond as his font of choice (the change was largely due to his aging eye sight) and most notably, he meticulously dated each poem in bold at the top, often using it as a substitute title. Dating each of his poems ended up being much more than his signature, however – the dates not only give an easy chronology to his evolution as a poet, but they reveal so much about the way he worked. Sean set himself the goal of writing "one good poem a day" and the dates reveal that he was, in fact writing daily. Some days he'd crank out two or three short ones, and some days he'd rework something to "make it good." He'd also established a routine of sharing his poems with a small group of trusted readers, and I was among these readers for the last 30 years, receiving monthly or even weekly letters through the 1990s, and then almost daily emails thereafter, showing his latest work.

Keeping with tradition, Sean started emailing me his poems for The Doctor Series as he wrote them, followed often by subtle revisions days later. We'd already spoken on the phone at length, and I was, of course, already aware of his diagnosis, the proposed treatment plan, and his mindset in the face of all this – but I wasn't fully prepared for his gloves off approach to his situation, which came pouring out in his poems. I couldn't read all of them in real time; they were too painful, too close. I was talking to Sean nearly every day at that point, and I needed to stay buoyant, for my own sake if not his.

At a time when most people might have "taken a break" from writing, having just been diagnosed with a rapacious cancer and immediately whipped into a dizzying regimen of doctor appointments and medical procedures, Sean instead did what he'd always done: he dove headfirst into the subject before him. He began to tear open the universe as his own world was being ripped apart, and he used the opportunity to explore what it means to fight to stay alive, not only for oneself, but for the ones we love.

Early on in the series, Sean equates his cancer with "the angry demons/in my gut/in my liver.../I picture them/sneering, claws/embedded/hiding inside/and I hope they get half/this hell" (Part 7). This is one of many references in this collection to cancer as a demon or monster taking over his body. This is how Sean chose to understand what was happening to him and how he chose to fight it.

There's also a strong comic book sensibility in The Doctor Series, from "action hero/fireworks" at the end of Part 2, to his reference to Aquaman in Part 45, or "I'm heroing up" in Part 58. Sean was an avid reader of comics, so it's no wonder. Super heroes and action heroes populated his poetic landscape because they alone held the power to vanquish the monsters threatening him from under his bed, hiding in his closet, hovering above him as he slept, devouring him from the inside. So it was a natural impulse for him to call upon this imagery in his fight against the demon Cancer, but he never lost sight of the odds: "Bruce Lee/I am bringing/fists/to a gun fight/and/I/might/die" (Part 13), and it is this constant awareness of the stakes at play that make these poems and this collection so penetratingly beautiful.

We see numerous allusions to boxing in this collection as well. He likens his rounds of chemo to rounds in a boxing ring, fighting Death and his demons, lifting himself off the mat from yet another losing match. In Part 23, we see him in training, counting pushups with the names of his wife and daughter, preparing for another losing round of nauseating drugs pumped through his veins:

Contaminated me:
I am
working the floor,
pushing against the earth
only
eighty times,
I push against the drugs,
each push,
a shove,
a shotgun blast
against the
sinister fatigue,
at the end
everything in me
is tight,
my mind like a wheel,
fury trembling through
the last pushes,
circles of water
drop from my eyes
to the blue mat beneath me,

eighty-one,
Cecilia,
eighty-two,
Tess,
eighty-three,
did not
sign up,
eighty-four

for this,

eighty-five,

I let go,

fall

and wonder on the floor

if I would work

so hard

if it was

just me.

Part 31 brings us back to the ring:

Each day

before I go in the ring

I cry so hard I curl,

then I undo

relying on no one,

a stretch

and then I'm ready to unload

a giant laser cannon of rage,

usually

fully loaded

between 9:30 and 10:30

each day

The Doctor Series, then, is the chronicle of Sean Flaherty's last, brave, bloody-knuckled fight for his life. We come back to the familiar themes: death, disappointment, betrayal, loss, and love. But unlike Sean's earlier clashes with these themes, this last engagement provides a gut-wrenching view from ringside, because we're as aware as Sean is that this is truly a life or death struggle. And because of Sean's own idiosyncrasies – the chronological ordering of his poems and the immediate, deeply focused personal perspective, we find ourselves struggling with him in real time through his last eight months, wondering at every turn whether this will be the last round, whether this story will have a happy ending. There is love and anger, humor, fear, deep personal insight, bravery, and self-mocking pride as Sean enters the ring every day, armed to the teeth and kicking back at Death and his pet demon Cancer with all the super hero strength he can muster. Sean explores everything from the mundane trickle of 5-FU through his IV to fantastical leaps of imagination, full of explosions and magic and the possibility of winning in the end, but it's his clear determination to fight that comes through in every page.

I cry I love you,
I cry,
afraid of the pain,
I have every intention,
will do
my level best
to go into
every round
throwing
solid punches,
to come out
on top,
to keep fighting
with
all my will,
to be
on my feet
when it's over.

Sean opened himself up in the most private, intimate ways for us all to know exactly what he was up against and what his hopes, fears, victories, and pains were. Yet he also wasn't afraid to take a hard look at himself in the work, as if he were suddenly seeing beyond his own pumped-up, superhero identity to the frail dying man behind the mask: "If only/I could/show you/the scary,/angry,/lonely,/disturbing/faces /behind/the brave one/I/always wear." (Part 41).

There were times when I had to look away from it all, and he understood; he forgave me for that, because he knew it was a difficult and bloody fight, hard to watch, but he never gave up. He kept right on swinging, focused on the next round immediately in front of him: "the quickest glimpse/too far forward/is a tidal wave of drowning sand…" (Part 60). I would read some of The Doctor Series immediately and respond immediately with praise and awe – for they were awe-inspiring to me – while some I stowed away to read later, when I was feeling stronger.

It's difficult to pick a favorite from among the 97 poems in this series. There are several, though, that really hit me in the gut and stuck with me long after reading. These include: Parts 25, 38, 50, 53, 68, 77, 65, 66, and 97. What strikes me most about this collection is Sean's own recognition of his declining situation and the shift in things he thinks about most as he begins to tally his losing rounds. He thinks about his neighbors and his neighborhood; he muses on how his wife and daughter will fare when he's gone; he spews anger at the callousness of one of his physicians; he rallies up while feeling strong and starts to imagine a future where e's a survivor; he makes plans beyond the next hospital visit. Through the roller coaster ride of Sean's own insights into his prognosis, we follow his journey from his crippling claustrophobia in a PET scanner, to his detailed descriptions of otherwise routine daily movements (shaving, dressing himself), through his anger and denial ("the toughest son of a bitch ever to dream in my head/daring me,/if I don't look into the mirror/then I can forget I have cancer/but I look/and dream today/you're going/to live) and finally, to the unfiltered recognition of his plight, with the awful realization and his final written words, "I am dying."

Over thirty years of sharing our writing with each other, doing public readings, attending residencies, submitting grants, and printing chapbooks, we always encouraged each other to do our best work – but most of all to find the right balance in life that allowed us to keep writing even as life got in the way (family, jobs, kids, marriage – all the usual things that might stop us), and to this end I tip my hat to Sean. He never stopped writing; he produced some of the best poetry I've ever read; he explored the very heart and soul of what it means to want to live; and even in the face of death, he kept right on swinging to the end.

One final note about The Doctor Series: Sean was a big fan of collaboration, from joint readings over the years with fellow writers Shay Totten, Bowman Hastie, John Shahnazarian, Patrick Murray, Peter Dinklage, and myself, among many others, to printed chapbooks and flyers that included illustrations by artists he wanted to support (Skinny White Beer Machine, The Love Boat, Cannibal Love, etc.), to his final collaboration with Ciaran Parr for this book – Ciaran began illustrating the collection while Sean was still in the fight, and his beautiful illustrations are hauntingly apt for the last words of Sean Flaherty.

Ciaran Cooper
March 14, 2017

The Doctor Series

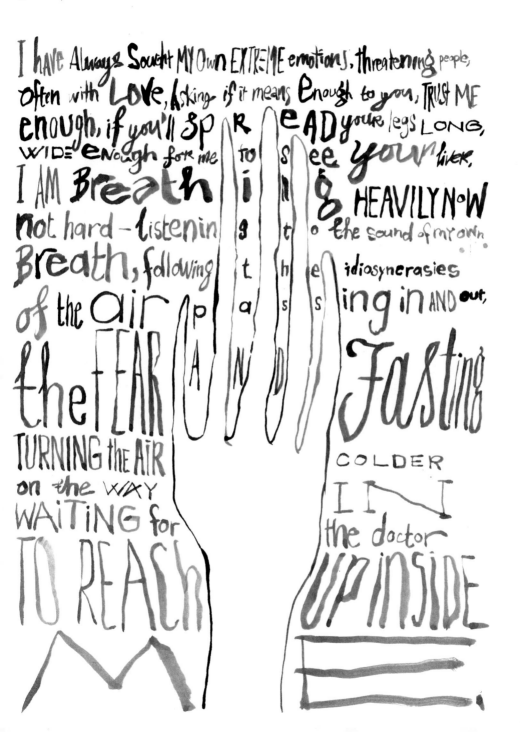

I have Always Sought MY Own EXTREME emotions, threatening people, often with LOVE, Asking if it means Enough to you, TRUST ME enough, if you'll SP R EAD your legs LONG, WIDE enough for me to see your liver,

I AM Breathing HEAVILY NOW not hard - listenin g t o the sound of my own Breath, following t h e idiosyncrasies of the air p a s s ing in AND out,

the FEAR A N D Fasting

TURNING the AIR on the way COLDER I N

WAITING for the doctor

TO REACH UP INSIDE

ME

9 May 2014

The Doctor,
Part 1

I have always sought
my own
extreme
emotions,
threatening people,
often
with love,
asking if it means
enough
to you,
do you
trust me
enough,
if you'll spread your legs long,
wide enough
for me to see
your liver,
I am breathing
heavily now –
not hard –
listening to the sound of my own breath,
following the
idiosyncrasies
of the air
passing
in and out,
the fear and fasting
turning the air
colder
on the way
in
waiting for the doctor
to reach up inside me.

12 May 2014

The Doctor, Part 2

I pretend
it is a multi-million dollar
secret,
a microfilm
in high demand
on the black market
hidden deep
in my belly,

the doctor pokes me,
prods me,
points
and says,
"cancer,"

like he's a
double agent,
like I'm
the gingerbread man,
I jump from the table
and, wearing only
my hospital gown,
my bare feet
padding the tarmac,

I'm running down the street just as fast as I can,
racing past
signs,
past
windows filled with
life,
want, want, want, want,
I want, I want
to eat
everything,
to steal all the jewelry,
I want
to have sex
with everyone I see,
smashing through the glass:

action hero
fireworks.

ALL (RED) Star Must Be Shot From Card To WIN

22 May 2014

The Doctor, Part 3

Young
Coney Island rides,
I get used to appointments –
I can,
with gunshy butterflies,
shoot out the star –
but I'm afraid to get on
the throwup machine
because I've been on before,
my face pressed against
bloody fingerprints
spotting the entrance to the cave
of the PET
and I always like to say
that I still like
to ride the rides
that scare me most.

22 May 2014
The Doctor, Part 4

Trying not to shake,
standing naked
in the middle of the room,
arms wide
I stretch
and begin to
assess

what
I get
to keep.

24 May 2014

The Doctor, Part 5

Three weeks ago
I was a skinny white
beer machine,
I was
walking briskly
everywhere,
I was
past the dream of a soft gray
v-neck sweater
scooping a trowel into the fresh soil
in any garden morning,
I was living
the hard cruise control
of modern survival,

now I am flat,
a broken machine,
my back on a black
Tempur-Pedic mattress,

the room is cold,
because hospitals—the only evidence
of the 21st Century –
are always
cold,

I am staring at the ceiling
again,
my eyes melting
in the bright
surgery light,
my stomach
another
panic twist,

They call
the morphine
twilight:

my mouth
is a warrior
for the word.

26 May 2014
The Doctor,
Part 6

If only
all the love
could ambien
the irrational fear,
the ancient monster,
the overwhelming,
suffocating tentacles
swooping down
when the safe blanket
keeps slipping off the bed,
it surrounds you and says
if you close your eyes
no matter
how many nights
there was no sleep,
it says
if you close them now,
if you try to sleep
you won't open them again,
harbinger grades of gray
coloring the way
to black, black, black.

30 May 2014
the doctor Part 7

Feel it on my
fingers,
I can smell the
poison
worse
than the worst
hangover
sweat,
the toxins
blossom
aglow
in my nose —
I can smell
everything.
Wicked
good...
maybe even better—

AND I can tell
from the ozone of sm
this shit,
this ~~shit~~ is
some bad juju.

I am different now
I am not sure
what I'm suppo
but its different
and while they're
really sick
I think about
in my gut,
in my liver...
I picture them

Stomach

HELL

hell

be yet
...ing me
...ngry demons

...rings claws embedded, hiding inside and I hope they get

half this

30 May 2014
The Doctor, Part 7

Feel it on my fingers,
I can smell the poison
worse
than the worst
hangover sweat,

the toxins
blossom
aglow
in my nose –

I can smell
everything
wicked good,
maybe even better –

and I can tell
from the ozone of the smell
this shit,
this is
some bad juju:

I am different now,
I'm not sure
what I'm supposed to be yet
but it's different
and while they're making me
really sick
I think about the angry demons
in my gut,
in my liver,
I picture them
sneering, claws
embedded,
hiding inside
and I hope they get half
this hell.

2 June 2014

The Doctor, Part 8

The internet
is so
considerate

reaching out to me
through its electric reeds
compassionately
divining my future needs:

since my diagnosis a few week ago,
unsolicited
bulk
messages
have started to come
wearing the alluring hands of a clever carney,
cotton candy splayed big-tent, popcorn-smile wide
offering
number 24-525663
a term life policy,
seven hundred and fifty thousand dollars in coverage
(no exam needed),
a gratis policy review,
the enticement of
"simplified
protection"
or
magical-sounding
anti-aging tips
and, of course,
to stay focused on the big picture,
the promise of
peace of mind
that only
burial insurance can bring.

2 June 2014

The Doctor, Part 9

When I saw you on the street
today
I ran
multiple
diagnostics,
examined the results
against
the baselines
and,
after making some assessments,

my cancer,
MY
cancer
does not change
the datum
that
you still suck.

4 June 2014

The Doctor, Part 10

Writing my name
on the pages
of a hurried will,
it is hard
not to hear
the panting
of my mortality:

if
my life is ending
then to pore and pore
over
pictures of living,
friends,
my small family,

the way
the plastic coating
shines on the snapshots
under the glow
from the patina green banker's lamp
on the desk my father owned,

everyone captured on film
at truly
their very happiest,
the lights in the rooms
where the pictures
were taken
licking the world
with
a flash of gossamer,
I finally look
like a movie star
to me.

6 June 2014
The Doctor PART 11

FUNNY
FUNNY THING
WALKING by
the guillotine
is that you get to STOP
for a moment To see everyone you've
been WANT-   ing to see
EVER since   that FINALLY a solid JOB
EVER   since THAT
WILDLY FALLing AND
FALLing in LOVE
WITH THE BEST thing
THAT'S EVER HAPPENED
IN A BAR
EVER SINCE that KID
EVER SINCE, EVER SINCE,
but
NOTHING
cripples me more,
MAKES Me Shatner's
KIRK ZAPPED with

SOME BETTER THAN A PHASER
ALIEN BEAM of

All This Fucking Love

HAS ME CRYING like the RAIN outside

Because, SAVAGE WARRIOR poet

angry asshole I AM I NEVER KNEW
I had that much AND like the odds I won't look
up ALL MY OLD animal friends

DISNEY delicate walking up slowly,
PETTING THE flies AWAY, catching my dinner
making sure I drink FIRST, Giving me what
they could have HAD, it's another TELL that THIS IS

REALLY THAT BAD.

t,
to the FLOOR,
KNEES
D AND SCARED

6 June 2014
The Doctor,
Part 11

Funny,
funny thing
walking by
the guillotine
is that you get to stop for a moment
to see everyone you've been wanting to see
ever since that
finally a solid
job,
ever since that
wildly falling and falling in love with the best thing that's ever happened in
a bar,
ever since
that kid,
ever since,
ever since,
but
NOTHING cripples me more,
makes me Shatner's Kirk zapped
with some
better than a phaser
alien beam of sonic delight,

drops me to the floor,
on my knees
good and scared
all this fucking love
has me crying
like the rain outside
because,
savage warrior poet angry ass-hole I am
I never knew
I had that much
and,
like the odds I won't look up,
all my
old animal friends
Disney delicate
walking up slowly,
petting the flies away,
catching my dinner,
making sure I drink first,
giving me
what they could have had,
it's another tell
that this is really that bad.

10 June 2014

The Doctor, Part 12

Cancer,
cancer,
cancer
like a whammy on a witch with my wand
I am extremely,
expulsively,
exponentially
pugilistic
and open
about it
and,
as some rise to the occasion
I was sorry to see
it took all this:
ten years and
your finding out
to bring back the book you borrowed.

11 June 2014
The Doctor, Part 13

Strapped
to an Evian bottle
pumping
5-FU
through
a thin, clear plastic,
length of my arm
tube
into me,
Bruce Lee,
I am bringing
fists
to a gunfight
and
I
might
die.

No one has said that
and I talked a long time
to my neighbor
on my black, diamond-plate stoop
as the steamy, gray clouds covered the stars
in last night's swampy Brooklyn
we talked about
missing bullets,

this sweet kid from Tucson
who went over
a soldier
and
didn't die,
another
lucky roadsign –

people
google and cringe,
I jig and shimmy,
I vault,
over that evil Alice Fucking Rabbithole,
I keep
moving –
serpentine,
faking,
dodging,
loading my punches

looking for an opening.

13 June 2014
The Doctor,
Part 14

Got a
lightning scar,
a bleached
zap
on my helmet
where some of this radioactive
crap
splashed out the side of my tiny muppet mouth
along with all the
other drugs:

if I stop
I'm not sure
what I'm doing,
I watch me
following
signs,
directions,
instructions,
arrows,

keep moving,
keep moving,
race
to the next
appointment,
to the next
doctor,
the next
script,

race
out of the now
and into the next –

they prescribed
Xanax,
the white label on the light brown bottle says
alprazolam,
point five milligrams
for racing thoughts

but I like
my thoughts
to race,

long as they don't close in,

and when they creep up
like they do,
(quiet in the dark)
I leave the bottle
in my red, cross-shaped
medicine chest
with all the other
new bottles
and stretch out
like a straight blue line
in the middle of the floor
listening to the air move
from the rain outside the window
and into the room
again and again,
listening to my wife and daughter
shuffling, rolling,
kicking at sleep in their rooms,
the soundtrack
for thoughts
to race to,

point five milligrams
of life.

14 June 2014
The Doctor,
Part 15

Outside my body,
speckled on my skin,
the warmth of my own blood is a blanket
so flay me,
you fuck,
the way Karloff
slices up Lugosi
in the end of "The Black Cat,"
slice me
with those ten thousand
small cuts,
reach down my throat
and rip up my insides,
shove a pencil into my urethra
and break it,
smash my innards,
pummel
my soft parts,
waterboard me
with lightshafts of radiation
until I tire you down
because
I can take it,
I can take it,
I can take it
with a smile
that says
I have never wanted so badly to feel my fingers around a throat
and I'll beg even once:
please,
don't take
my daughter's father
because the universe
will never forgive me.

Toying Slumber

I shot from HIGH OFF THE GROUND I WAS in an office on ~~101~~ first AVENUE seat

Fluorescent LIGHTS shimmer dim AND dull behind shiny METALLIC

And the DOCTOR behind the desk, stern and seri

Another doctor chimes in,

it's Malignant AND the

CANCER

has

Spread

to your

Liver

through your

Lymph nodes. there is an ugly, clear glass paperweight on

LAST GUYS WHO SAT HERE,

In The Dream I am Forty-Seven, Very, Very Happily ma

Little four-and-a-half year old thrust from my Babbit rut

TRENCHES INTO the horrible Theater of Lonel

and I cannot

Escape the Echoes of

rrible dream:

to my wife — EMBEDDED in the ceiling *the Awful*
fixtures that look *like* handled frames used in old ice trays —
he says you→ have a tumor an **Angry** tumor,

YOU
ying
IFE

the SIZE of a brick INSCRIBED   from one of the

a Beautiful
safe I
AR
rock.

BEACHES

16 June 2014
The Doctor,
Part 16

Toying slumber
I shot from a terrible dream:

high off the ground
I was in an office
on First Avenue
seated next to my wife –

embedded in the ceiling
the awful
fluorescent lights
shimmer dim and dull behind shiny
metallic plastic fixtures
that look like the handled frames used in old ice trays –

and the doctor
behind the desk,
stern, serious
he says
you have a tumor,

an angry tumor
another doctor chimes in,

it's malignant
and the cancer
has spread
to your liver
through your
lymph nodes,

there is an ugly, clear glass paperweight
on his desk
the size of a brick
inscribed
"thank you
for saving
my life"
from one
of the last guys
who sat here,

in the dream
I am forty-seven,
very,
very happily
married
with a beautiful little four-and-a-half year old
thrust from my Babbitt rut
over the safe trenches
into
the horrible theater of lonely war
and I cannot
escape
the echoes
of shock.

16 June 2014
The Doctor,
Part 17

The comb smoothing through the mirror
I imagined
a
taxidermist,
a
coroner,
a
mortician
pushing my hairs straight,

the shaving cream colder on my skin,
I suck a mean, tough guy drag off a joint
thinking about
some stranger's grandma
on a plane to Florida a few years ago
when she tried to sell me
her god shit
I told her
I'm sorry I don't believe in god
smiling my smile
and she was sad
when she said I was going to hell,

I turn her
into my mortician
as I scrape the razor
over the straight bone on the left side of my jaw,
lean my head back a little
and ease the dragon smoke out my nose

into her face,
caterpillar plumes
swirling under her unbelieving eyes
and I tell them,
smiling my smile,
I put on
a shirt with buttons,
a crisp collar,
(I turn it up),
I tell
my coroner,
my
taxidermist, my mortician, my
somebody else's grandma
I'm gonna be
just fine,
I'm gonna be
beautiful
if my head is on a cold metal table
or high
in the upper flourishes
of anybody's hell.

18 June 2014
The Doctor,
Part 18

I
can't
change
that
right
now.

18 June 2014
The Doctor,
Part 19

Haunting my life
walking by the edge of a river
I might not see in a year,
I am a ghost,
hoping,

there is a monster inside of me
and cancer is like the worst love:

thrust
into
possible futures,
the pain,
the unexpected, prolonged, complete
agony of a broken heart
a fairly even match
for the awful chemicals
gargling my organs,

when the pain is
everywhere
you live again and again
like the victim of a terrible accident
mapping routes
like ghosts get
a next time
to avoid certain tragedy,
to avoid
I can't change that right now
destiny.

18 June 2014
The Doctor,
Part 20

A call
from the right place
I suppose,
a long distance
motherfucker
jammed my signal,

shook me
with the words
"miracle doctor,"

with the words
"miracle cure,"
with the words,
"if you were my son
I'd fly you to
Las Cruces
tomorrow"

jolted
my fear,
made me check my
balance
and
pissed me
off.

18 June 2014

The Doctor,
Part 21

Traveling into the future can be dangerous:

at first,
ordinary things
begin to
disappear –
neighbors,
cats,
stop signs,
streets –

then the things in my home,
the sunflowers I brought for Cecilia,
the little red wind-up robot I bought for Tess,
everything I love
begins to disintegrate,
falling away
to dust

leaving me alone
in a very big, empty room
with only the sound of my
eyelids
clicking
open and shut
for comfort.

20 June 2014
The Doctor, Part 22

Like some king angel
so many people
ask
what they can do

and I've thought of something:

if you're going to
research
my odds
to survive

please
keep that
close to
your chest.

20 June 2014

The Doctor,
Part 23

Contaminated me:

I am
working the floor,
pushing against the earth
only
eighty times,

I push against the drugs,
each push,
a shove,
a shotgun blast
against the
sinister fatigue,
at the end
everything in me
is tight,
my mind like a wheel,
fury trembling through
the last pushes,
circles of water
drop from my eyes
to the blue mat beneath me,

eighty-one,
Cecilia,
eighty-two,
Tess,
eighty-three,
did not
sign up,
eighty-four
for this,
eighty-five,

I let go,
fall
and wonder on the floor
if I would work
so hard
if it was
just me.

20 June 2014

The Doctor,
Part 24

Unsatisfied
I am mortal
I run through my nine lives:
the time I was under
sixteen boots,
eight
wilding puppies
from Queens
trying to snuff me out
in 1990,
the times I tricked it,
on a skateboard
inches away from the bottom of eighteen wheels
in 1989,
the times
no one knows about
in a car
I was driving
like a skateboard
as fast as I could
under the mushroom mountain fogs
through the Henry Hudson
LSD tunnels
and all along the vodka curves
of the northeast coast,

I count the ways
I could have died
by now
and laugh
at this joke —

it's one of those jokes
that gives the illusion
of going in a circle:

May 1st, I passed my first
kidney stone,
the next
Tuesday, May 6th,
I had a catscan
to make sure the cats
and the stones were all gone,
Wednesday, May 7th,
Doctor Daryl called and said the stones were gone
but something
about the cats
bothered him
and that Doctor Bart
was waiting for my call,
Thursday, May 8th,
Doctor Bart performed a colonoscopy
and told very druggedy me
there was a tumor
and it was malignant
and that Doctor Mitch, The Surgeon
was waiting for my call,
May 9th, Friday,
Doctor Mitch asked why I thought I was here
and explained
the shit had moved on in,

metastasized like mustard
to my sweet, sweet liver
(hold the onions) and ordered
a PET scan
to go,
May 14th
Dr. Mitch
confirmed
the wurst
and said Dr. Pillsbury,
the oncologist
was waiting for my call
and we met on Tuesday, May 20th
when Dr. Pillsbury
notched it up,
Stage IV,
confirmed,
confirmed
without a kidney stone
to say
hey look at me!
just dead
in three years,
I stopped laughing,
stopped breathing,
stared through the
ninth floor window
and admired the roof decks
in the courtyard
below.

24 June 2014
The Doctor,
Part 25

Already
deadly
rabbit white
my skin burns
faster now
so I am supposed to
refrain
from
walking in the sun,

the heat an hour away
I called my mother
who asked how I was
I said I'm walking along the river
she said
wiseass
I said
I think I might die
because it was
top
of mind,
I was working my way
through a short tail
of a cold kind of
PTSD
and I couldn't stop
thinking
the Creepiest Thought,

the shawl she knit
over the phone
was made with a very
fine-tuned,

practiced pattern
colored with splashes
of WASP denial:

we're all
going to die
she Jedi-ed,

I inserted
but I mean
maybe soon,
sooner
than I had perhaps
planned or
hoped,

she comforted,
I think about that sometimes,
what if I
or anyone
gets hit
by a truck
or a car
while crossing the street
one day?,

I told her
I have the license plate
of the truck,
I know the name
of the driver,
I even know
when he's coming down the road.

25 June 2014
The Doctor,
Part 26

I am drinking a beer with my chemo,
the balloon bottle
at my side
pumping 5-FU
through
the wristwatch
buried in my chest,

the steroids
got me
ghost rider
speeding,

I'm in a bar
called
Skinny Dennis –
it used to be a café
owned by two Turkish twins –

the crash is coming,
the crash is coming,
I can feel the tires
losing their teeth,

the crash is coming
but for now
I am so hard
wired
I want to bite my arm off,

maybe
another beer
and
tell your husband
tonight
I think you're beautiful,
tell him
I love you.

27 June 2014

The Doctor, Part 27

*"Imagine there's no heaven.
It's easy if you try."*
— John Lennon

I've been
on the ground before,
picked myself up
out a puddle of my own blood,
I've been
attacked,
eight kids tried to kill me one night,
I made it
twenty seven years ago
I grabbed ALL my shit
laying in the middle of Broadway,
these fuckers'
field goal attempts
on my head,
my ribs,
and with the fear
the pain doesn't feel real,
you can't believe
someone else
would do this to you,
on your back,
upside down
like you're being cooked alive,
a smash in the side
is almost funny
until you can't breathe anymore,

I ran like a bear on fire to catch a
moving cab
going north
and spent ten years
living it again and again,
all the things
I didn't do,
a snub nose duct-taped to the bottom
of my skateboard
(the big one with the giant shark),
taking
a bit bite
out of someone's cheek,
smashing at least one of them
in the face with the board,
the metal trucks
dislodging several
gold teeth,
blood exploding
back towards Duane Street –

I don't hesitate:

like the earth
I have nothing
but terrible stories
about religion

but right now
I'd take a heaven,
a chance
to hold my dad,
chat with him
about crazy for a moment,
catch up

with all my love
for my Henry,
I'd tell Ginsberg
I'm sorry
I didn't go
to the Clemente show
that perfect summer day
Madison Avenue
nauseous with the smell of linden trees
with you
'cause I thought
you were trying
to fuck me,

I'd drive to
the house on Pleasant Street
where my maternal
grandmother
lives,
Tess,
tell her
I did okay,
maybe a little better
and named the angel I call my
daughter
after her.

29 June 2014
The Doctor,
Part 28

Uphill,
everything
feels awful,
sirens
banshees
echoing up the blocks
all around the hospital,

sunk
deep
into my head
my eyes
dart the room,
spinning wheels,
scratching claws,
a bird
flying hard
against shuttered windows,

please,
I peel back a smile
and whisper to the nurse like my lover,
please
get me
the fuck
out,

I don't
want
to do this
anymore.

30 June 2014
The Doctor,
Part 29

Assaulted by
daily threats
my new rage
is overloaded.

After a good cry
I think about
this ass-hole
who says he's going to take
my kid
and I experience
a cataclysmic nuclear explosion,
I go
full nova:

sure
everything is harder to do,

I shit
cinderella cancer
cinderblocks
covered in
spiny cloves,
construction site
orange and clove
christmas pomander balls
that hurt so much
I want a Quaalude
after the dance,

at times
it takes
murky, cursing at pain
hours
to unlock myself,

unseat
myself,
to Lazarus

and I walk through dream soup –

when you're moving
so
sluggishly
you play chess
in the mirror,
anything
but the truth
a bad move

and the one move that
eludes me,
the chance
to face
the minotaur,
MY
minotaur
slipped away,
my revenge,
my honesty
robbed –

I hate
what my stepfather
did
to children,
animals,
the women
who loved him,

what I saw him do,
what I know
he did
and he
got away with it,
swept away
in the blind chaos
of St. Alzheimer's,

saved
from me,

everyone
says his
new wife,
the one who lives in that
new
hell house
the one who doesn't know
about the
old
hell house
is so nice
she doesn't need to know
what an evil,
evil man he was, Sean
and it reminds me of people who say
to my cancer
"be positive"
"stay positive"
"focus on being fucking positive"
when I have a hand,
fingers creep
creeping around my throat
that feel

an awful lot
like my stepfather's hand
when he grabbed me
by the throat,

it is
DAMNING
I
never
get to see the look,
the mean now
wiped blank I
never get
that truth chess move
when he
gets it,
that
I want him
hurting

and now
breaking his jaw,
plunging
a steak knife
into him

has all the
magic
satisfaction
of filling a pillow case
with dog shit
to
stab and punch.

2 July 2014

The Doctor,
Part 30

Sick of being
prepared
like the feature
victim
in a survival-horror
film,

I am sick
of being
prepared
with nothing
but
synthetics,

saturated in synthetics
slowing me down,

thank you
for being
my Magnificent Seven,
my hero
who shows up
at the last minute
when my fingers are
slipping off the edge,

thank you
for locking me up
when I turn
into worse than a werewolf
ready to shred
the first
wrong word,

thank you
for being
my best friend,
I'm glad we
haven't been married
long enough
to kill each other
in a late, long, mean corridor,

I'm glad there's
so much
fresh blood between us
that we're still enjoying
all the new flavors,
new meals,
the occasional
new look,
new feels,
new love,
so much
still new
advancing
impudently
into the hot face
of mortality
becomes
easier
in the vague, rare, singular comfort
of trust.

7 July 2014
The Doctor,
Part 31

Each day
before I go in the ring
I cry so hard I curl,

then I undo
relying on no one,
a stretch
and then I'm ready to unload
a giant laser cannon of rage,
usually
fully loaded
between 9:30 and 10:30
each day,

I sit on the stoop
a lot these days
breathing slow, green-blue smoke down the sidewalk,
cooling,
easing
down
after retching
up,
after twisting
up,

I catch
the odd look,
the odd sniff
of passersby,
some
living close by,

I sweep
to keep it clean,
to keep
the rats away,

each day
since they opened across the street
at 106
North First Street,
The Journal Gallery –
either
that tall giraffe
Thurston Moore Wannabe
hipster schtoon
that owns the place
who was probably
really good
at selling coke to his friends in college
or one of his
underpaid –
dumps their garbage
on top of our garbage,

on Thursday
a very nice girl
in a very nice dress
dropped
The Journal Gallery's
bag of garbage
on top of the bags and bags of garbage
in front of our building
and walked
very pretty
back across the street,

I followed her
like a cancer cop
just like the shitters before her
who left their dog shit in front of my apartment in 1993
who I followed
all over Brooklyn
with their three-legged dog's shit
in a bag I was holding
asking why did you leave your dog's shit in front of my apartment?

I walked into the gallery
and said,
excuse me,
you've been dumping your trash in front of my building
each day
and it isn't very neighborly,

eyes wide she snatched at
I'm just following orders,

I thought of the Nazis
and said,
it's not cool,

from the hip she
pushed the button:
does
just a little more garbage
really matter?

I said
hey,
I'm trying to keep the front of our building clean,
I'm fighting cancer
so I'm spending more time
there
and it just isn't a very neighborly thing to do
which is why it's probably
illegal
so please
stop,
thanks,
have a good day,

my shoulders walked out the door
before I did,
across the street
in my dark apartment
I smoked hard
to bring them back down
and saw her, her
shoulders
across the street
heaving
up and down

Audrey Hepburn at the end of the movie
and she
saw me,
our eyes locked,
both shamed
through my window
and fled,

oh.
shit. I have to fix
my karma
now,
asap,
I fumbled
for
something beautiful,
not offensive,
not too
sexy,
not too
little,
I fumbled,
I mumbled to my keys

and found her,

sorry,
I am so sorry to level that at you,
I am so sorry,
I didn't want
to hurt you,
you're right she said,
she smiled
at my sorries and said I've lost a lot of people
to cancer,

I said
your penis of a boss
needs a bucket of my wrath,
not you,
take this,

I handed her a penny-cube,
a cube
not too little,
not too
sexy
made of pennies
chromed
shiny silver
with a bouncy nugget inside
so it dings,

I said
the guy that made this
is someone,

I'm not anything,
I'm sorry
I'm just
the ass-hole across the street.

7 July 2014
The Doctor,
Part 32

My friend loves me:
when he finds out
I'm sick
he offers me everything,
he
baitsandswitches
saying let's have dinner,
brother,
with the others
and
like a good, crazy host
instead
lays out
cocaine
and
throws
hookers at me
who try to
poke me
like my doctors,

the last two things I want
(I said yes
and
I said no,
don't touch that
but you can rub my neck),

when I am done

telling everyone

high

how high

I love my wife,

high love,

more than ever,

my friend

rolls around with the girls,

sex trafficking

and we go to dinner in Chinatown

where the restaurant

is black and red and

reminds me of the club in Scarface,

The Babylon,

the coke makes me cold,

superaware

all I can smell

is gasoline as strong as the smell of iron

in blood

from the cocaine

process

and a little bit of perfume

is a girl

who told me and I didn't believe her before I was done asking

her name

is Valery Nicole,

my stomach

trying to make the dumplings

into something good.

7 July 2014
The Doctor,
Part 33

I feel good,
I get scared shitless,
I feel really good,
bouncing on my toes,
eyes forward,
faking with hints,
feints,
breathing into
my diaphragm,

I feel good,
really good,
ready to get torn up
just like last time,
probably
a little worse,

I get scared shitless
when I start to feel good again
because
it means
I have to go
back again,
that
it's Tuesday again,
the nurse, Jane,

Jane is going to stab me in the chest
gently
where the wristwatch is
with all that
poison
on top of the
poison
from the last time,

I feel good,
really good
today,
bouncing on my toes
the lights flashing,
I get near the ring,
ready
to go in one more time,
to take another
two weeks
of steady hits
before I feel good again.

8 July 2014

The Doctor, Part 34

Without them
I'm quite blind,
squinting at my street sign
like one of those
delicate
Europeans or Asians on a tour of
artisanal Brooklyn,

chemo gives me headaches
sometimes
when I wear
my glasses,

so
sometimes
I take them off
so not
to hurt my head,
so not
to see
the minutiae
in
the mirror,

I take them off
so I can't see
how bad it is,

I can pretend
I'm in a
dream or drugged fog

and when I go outside
I see
so poorly
it's a form of
anti-x-ray specs
backwards mask
everyone
blurred voices
and invisible features
as I hope they
see me.

10 July 2014
The Doctor,
Part 35

It is vicious, chemical vomiting,
the urge is not
like being sick,
drunk sick
fever sick,
you rise from your chamber sleep,
mouth agape,
frankensteining
purposefully to the opera pot,

it is an urgent suddenness,
the type of
human, animal trigger
belonging only
to medicine
and its darts,

the lack of control,
of participation
can be quite sad
unless you
adjust your perception
10x out,

this morning:
loud, round angry yawns of clear
bubbly
mucus and clear
bile,
spasms
exorcising
toxins,

lightheaded,
less Frankenstein
I take
one Zofran
for nausea,
one Atavan
for anxiety
and nausea,
roll two sizable cigarettes
selecting some sticky indica
to roll into the gumless rice paper
as opposed to a drier, headier strain
that could tap
the focus I need
to
teach the bull the cape
and at 4:15 I am
my eyes rocketing away from my body
as high into the sky as they can fly
looking for the moon,
I have propped the black metal door to our building
wide
casting the light
from the hallway fluorescents
onto the black bags of garbage and the clear bags of recycling
lined up to be collected on the pale sidewalk
open,

I am looking for the moon
or any planet
behind the clouds
exhaling long, elegant plumes
from my leonine mouth and nose
like the exhaust from an old factory
shooting lonely fire chimneys
reaching from their long into the dark sky
over Zug Island in Michigan
waiting to be
shut down for the night.

10 July 2014
The Doctor,
Part 36

You do terrible things,
one does
terrible things,
I have done terrible
things, made terrible
choices,
a clumsy storm,

there are the things I have survived
and the things
that have survived me,

there are also
amazing, beautiful,
loving things:
there is my
luck,
my unconditional
irreverence,
my child, my friends,
more
luck —

all of it
has to
add up,
it has to fit
into this
cancer
I have.

11 July 2014
The Doctor,
Part 37

Facebook
says
we're friends
but I'm not
convinced:

when we met
I was thirty
running from
expectations,
responsibilities
I needed
didn't want,

you were
nineteen, learning to
shoot stick,
to drink
in the pool bars
on the lower east side
like Lucy's,
you were
part of a
sloppy rock and roll song
ready to play
anywhere,
a frustrated gymnast
happy to cartwheel
in the trembling rafters
of the most dangerous places,

on 91,
my mom driving,
you dragged me
into the backseat on the highway

and then
into the
way back,
your freckles
tickling the rearview,
the road
lit up
ahead,

later,
after we all ate some mushrooms
you made out with my mom
in the front seat
and it was far away
and beautiful

but it put me off
and I ran past the locked gate out onto the
private property
and the beautiful cliffs along the coast
peeling my clothes off,
thinking the sun going down
and the exploding ocean
would take me in
now the mushrooms have changed me,
I'm more like them
than what was going on in the car,

I flashed barefoot naked a good mile,
a foggy string tied from my mind
to the pile of my clothes
back there,
I stopped
to itch my ass against
the top

of a good, sharp rock
jutting up,
I turned my head and smiled it felt so good
and saw a man
dressed for golf standing on his lawn
smoking his pipe
about the length of a golf club away from me
and my wild ass,

as the waves exploded behind my back
I turned away
like some kind of invisible bear I was driving
and in the cockpit I was saying,
I sure hope he doesn't call the cops
and holds onto this instead as some kind of
wild moment for him to share
over plates of trout
at dinner tonight
and the next summer

and all these summers later

we talk
because I'm sick,
you are an older
sloppy rock and roll song
and I can tell
when we talked today
I don't think we'd get along,
but, from here,
I can still
admire
your stupid American
anywhere redneck way.

After Obvious Lust

I WANT, I WOULD LIKE VERY BADLY TO BE YOUR H

on your Mother next to the EMPTY cu

Petals, and I

And All

of You

Be

so much less to wish for:

when I TURN TO ASH AND Mud, You ~~Need To~~ Quiet
, THE TWO of YOU Fold-ing over each other;
KNOW in my BONES
the Two
Will
Okay.

11 July 2014
The Doctor, Part 38

After obvious
lusts
there is
so much
less
to wish for:

I want,
I
would like
very badly
to be
your
hero
when I turn to ash
and mud,

you,
quiet
on your mother
next
to the
empty cushion,
the two of you
folding
over
each other,
petals,
and I know
in my bones
and all
the two of you
will be okay.

12 July 2014

The Doctor, Part 39

My hands don't feel like my hands,
they are smaller,
bonier,

most of the nurses smile
their pretty smile,
it hurts my doctor's face
to smile
her pretty smile,
they're all surprised
I don't have
mouth sores,
that I still have
my hair,

round four started Tuesday,
Thursday morning
there was a small, blue clamp
Nurse Jane forgot to remove
from the tube running the drugs
into the port
under my skin
beneath my clavicle,

I had to go back,
Jane sadly apologized
sincerely
oh we never leave these on
I'm so sorry,

so, unclamped, I am plugged into the bottle longer,
I have to
try
sleep,
wires and tapes and gadgets and tubes,
trying not
to roll over onto it,
trying not
to push any of it
over the side of the bed
onto the floor
for one more night,

I pace
away from the annoying sandman,
trying to
outlast
the dosage
so when the last drop
of 5-FU hits my port
I can be
awake
to untwist
the sinister shit
from one tube in my chest,
to flush the port with
a syringe,
to clean it
with another
and,
finally,
pull the needle out,
I wait like a hunter

but the nausea takes up
a lot of space in the blind,
it's either
the extra day
or round four
but a tornado of toxin
is twisting me up:
tonight,
each time I close my eyes
I am suddenly
sliding down the conveyor belt
into the hot, claustrophobic
PET scan coffin,
I become immediately
disoriented,
the drugs make me
extra sick,
junk sick,
motion in the part of your brain
that makes you sick,
I can't stop spinning,
my eyes
darting
to hold on
to a single point in the room,
my mouth open.

12 July 2014
The Doctor,
Part 40

I wrote that my hands
feel
unfamiliar,
the tips of my fingers
the skin,
the nerves around the tips
extra tender,

it hurts
to touch things,

the chemo
brain
makes me more
uneven,
it gives me a
fuzzy focus,
my equilibrium
a pendulum,

my stomach is a nuclear plant
best fed
cooling rods
and maybe some coconut water
because everything else is
shitting knives, is
a pummeling
in the corner,

all these side effects
have the eerie
side effect
of echoing
tortures
meant to raise
devils from men
and at my weakest,
face
down,
the sense of guilt,
the burden of my failure
is a powerful boot in my back
when I'm
getting ready
to push away
from the canvas
for another round.

12 July 2014
The Doctor,
Part 41

If only
I could
show you
the scary,
angry,
lonely,
disturbing
faces
behind
the brave one
I
always wear.

14 July 2014

The Doctor,
Part 42

"There ain't no Jesus gonna
come from the sky
Now that I found out
I know I can cry."
– "I Found Out" by John Lennon

The changes
are on,
I am a state of
devolve,

the bathroom,
a torture chamber,
Sean is
kneeling
at the pot,

I grab
the hair he still has
and smack him in the face,

where the fuck is the tough guy?!!,

I can't feel it,
I spit twice,
I can't feel it,

my voice is strained,
rough
when I yell
at myself,
it is a battle
to project,

the bathroom,
my pupa,
I cannot do
what I'm used to
and this
is only
round four,

I
struggle finding
my spark today,
I am
turning into
an
otherworldly
cancer
reptile:

my mouth is tight,
dry,
the lips are
numb from here,
the space
inside
smaller –

not like a place
you put food
anymore.

14 July 2014
The Doctor, Part 43

One friend
said he's afraid to see me
when I'm skinnier
at the end of the summer,
when I'm bald –
he looked away
while we ate,

one friend
invited me
and my cancer
over
for a barbecue
to get his
girlfriend back
(I told her
he's an ass
and he
got her back),

one friend
came to visit,
said
he'd done
the research
online,
he said
the odds
aren't good,

lots of
friends
won't tell me
but they
don't want to go
to the hospital
and
some friends
don't even call
and that's okay,
it's better
if they don't know
what to say.

14 July 2014
The Doctor,
Part 44

Like napping,
falling asleep alone,
a ball of a man
in the center of the bed,
the center
growing
heavier, the edges
of the bed
marching outwards
away
from the center,
the mass
quieting
everything,
so quiet
this
could be a way
to die.

14 July 2014
The Doctor,
Part 45

Sharks.
Sharks and
claustrophobia.
Now:
sharks,
claustrophobia and
cancer.

Other than losing
my daughter, my wife,
these things
terrify
me:

when I was twenty
I lived alone
in a small house
on a beach
and after a long Friday
in my carpenter's assistant
gig,
hauling lumber,
digging
postholes,
pounding and measuring,
I drove exhausted
to the video store
on a perfect summer night
and rented Jaws
on VHS,

after a few
Rolling Rocks
Brody and Hooper
were paddling
away from the shredded Orca
into the sunset
and I was carefully
placing
the mushrooms
my cousin had left
in the glove compartment
into my mouth,
chomping the heads off
first –

I walked through the door
with
the first rush,
grabbed a
flashlight
and headed to the water
even though
the moon
had turned
everything
blue,

curling sand
with my toes
I stared out
and out
hearing nothing,
removed my clothes
with
the next rush,
I looked up
to see if the stars
were alright with it
and I was
in the water,
up to my neck
fast,
remembering
very quickly
how to swim
vulnerable to
anything
for miles and miles,

I called out like Aquaman
sending psychic concentric circles
out
to all the living things,
an e-mail
to every
wiggly, creepy thing
and
a special dedication
went out
to
the sharks,

I splashed,
backstroking naked under the moon,
my body
perfect,
I swam
dangerous,
tapping
the rushes
for another length
until I was
arms heavy
tired,

on the beach
I got safe
in my clothes
and before I
turned
human again
I reached down
and howled,
calling
for a last splash,
finally:
a silver-white
fin to chase.

18 July 2014
The Doctor,
Part 46

You are the
very
least useful
person
on the team,

the go-to,
the
RN
for my oncologist,

our first meeting
you asked
where I work
and you said you lived
there
and had I heard about
that homeless guy
who's always around
Broadway and Houston,

he stabbed someone
you said
and you ran off
to print out a copy
of an article
for me,

I mentioned
pain,
fireballs of
pain
and your dull smile
said

I need to call you
when I am
in dolor,
that
you,
Tiffany,
will
help,
you said call,
you'd call right back to
help

and then you broke the rule,
the dating a high-school girl rule:
don't say you're going to call if you're
not going to call,

I called,
I trusted you
with my pain,
you never
called

and this week
I left a message
with
pain
details

and when you call
there is
dim
on the
other end,
blank,
nothing,
you haven't the
slightest
fucking idea
what I
need.

See you
Tuesday.

19 July 2014
The Doctor,
Part 47

I sing the body toxic:

the monsters
are growing
in number,
in size,

I draw pictures of monsters
and
after all this
they're growing,

riding in the front seat
with death
I am
eye to eye,
shoulder to shoulder
with the world,

each chemo,
each doctor
a little bit
a betrayal
from the west

and you
are the
master class
in western medicine,

I am healthy
and I don't get
how getting all this
sick,
my body
singed,
singing the body
toxic
is going to do
anything
but kill me,

I am
unafraid,
I am
ready
to die,

I do not
want
torture

and you,
the talking head of
The Cancer Factory,
Doctor Satan Segal
with your pale, pasty
ringless hands,
all the sex appeal of an open refrigerator door,

the
worst
energy
I've ever been near,
gentle as
an overpaid ape,
a
guessing monkey
with car keys,

you deliver
my doom:
you want
to put
a pump
pumping poison,
the size of a hockey puck
inside of me,
under my ribs
forever –

I thought
they caught
all the Nazis –

I'm ready to
die,
ass-hole
but my eyes
are still
beautiful,

when I left your office
and your
stupid,
painful arrows
to my future

my mind
dialed
Kevorkian

and I considered
my suicide
for the first time –

nothing gross
like my dad –

I'm ready
to die,
doctor ass-hole,
but not
jaundiced,
tricked out
with evil
tinker toys,

the terrible thing
about
memory
is I will
never
forget
your name –

and
n naming
there is
magic –

t is nice to
wake up,

I listen to
Jimmy Cliff,
The Harder They Come

and think about the east –

I will
never
kill
myself,

I will not
go gentle,

I will not
go ugly,
forever
sick.

THERE WAS NO CANCER WHEN I GOT UP TODAY, THE PANIC GONE, THE TEDIUM O
TERROR, I DID NOT VOMIT.

I SEDUCED MY BEAUTIFUL SLEEPING WIFE BEFORE THE STIRRING LITTLE FEET,

I MADE BREAKFAST MOVED AROUND THE HOUSE, FREE, SIDE-EFFECT FREE. DE
ABLE TO FEEL MY FINGERTIPS I DID NOT FUMBLE WITH BUTTONS DRESSING
BORINGLY INTACT,

OF IMMORTALITY MINE AGAIN, FREE OF POISONS, CHEMO, FREE OF SLEEPLESS

I LEAVE
FOR THAT DREAD RUT
THE JOYLESS
SUBWAY
AND,
DESCENDING THE STEPS,
I
Fred Astaire:
ONE
TWO,
CHA CHA CHA.

REE, STUBBING MY TOE ON THE CORNER   THE TABLE THE WORST PAIN,
TIED MY LACES WITHOUT LOOKING, MY   OF DIGNITY MY CONFIDENCE

24 July 2014
The Doctor,
Part 48

There was
no cancer
when I got up
today,

the panic
gone,

the tedium of the sun, of
immortality
mine again,

free of poisons, chemo, free of
sleepless
terror,
I did not vomit,

I seduced
my beautiful,
sleeping
wife
before the stirring
little feet,

I made breakfast,
moved
around the house,
free,
side-effect free,
depression free,
stubbing my toe
on the corner of
the coffee table
the worst pain,

able to feel my fingertips
I did not
fumble with buttons
dressing myself,

I tied
my laces
without looking,

my dignity,
my confidence
boringly
intact,

I leave
for that dread rut
the joyless
subway
and,
descending the steps,
I
Fred Astaire:

one
two,
cha cha cha.

30 JULY 2014
THE Doctor,
PART 49

It's Beautiful at five O'clock in July
in North Truro very close to the
tip of the Cape,
the wind does the breathing for you

Y
O
U,
the'
AIR,

the silence over the tree-line a Robin Leach Fantasy
A Caviar Dream. Walking Around the street side of—
I overhear My Wife on the phone saying we have to a
what if I lose my best friend, What if Tess loses her f
he lost his, what if—it feels like being at My funeral—
It's A door I could step through Where I could be a hopeless j
but I stick My chest out, Keep My Shit Togetta
with a life-affirming Smile, put myself on the right
the numbers, the Estimates the Studies, I cry I Love YOU,
I cry I Love You, I cry, Afraid of the pain, I have e
round throwing solid punches, to come ou
My feet when it's Over.

ssic Cape Cod cottage
the WORST
t the age

nd step BackWards before she sees me,
ntion, will do my level best to go into Every
r to keep fighting With ALL my Will, to be an

30 July 2014
The Doctor,
Part 49

It's beautiful at five o'clock in July
in North Truro
very close to the tip of
the Cape,

the wind does the breathing
for you,
the air,
the silence over the tree-line
a Robin Leach
fantasy,
a caviar dream,

walking around
the street side of
the classic Cape Cod cottage
I overhear
my wife on the phone
saying
we have to consider
the worst,
what if
I lose my best friend,
what if
Tess
loses her father
at the age
he lost his,
what if

– it feels like being at my funeral –

it is a door
I could step through
where I could be
a hopeless sponge

but I stick my chest
out,
keep my
shit
together
with a
life-affirming
smile,

put myself
on the right side of
the numbers,
the estimates,
the studies,

I cry I love you,
soldier
and step backwards
before she sees me,

I cry I love you,
I cry,
afraid of the pain,
I have every intention,
will do
my level best
to go into
every round
throwing
solid punches,
to come out
on top,
to keep fighting
with
all my will,
to be
on my feet
when it's over.

4 August 2014

The Doctor,
Part 50

Gasp in the dark
shooting the brain
awake!,
there's that panic,
along with its betrayal, the
discomfort,
the fear of
rotting,
waiting
for the torture,
for the rot –

DRUNK!,
I want to get wasted!,

I own my life,
I own
my death

but CANCER,
cancer is
the loneliest, most
unshareable
place I have ever been:

when I can get outside my head
I float in outer space,
a sudden
alien,
my home world
unfamiliar,

when I talk to people
I wear
a ten-mile stare
and I can see
in their eyes
where I am already gone
and look past that,

far away
I love you all
so much,
I'm sorry
I failed:

I will go,
my wife
will find
a healthy
husband
to hold her,
(maybe he'll even like
to dance),
another father
to love
our child,

I am packing,
moving to an island,
no phones,
no mail,
no
hospitals,
just sundowns.

5 August 2014
The Doctor, Part 51

Saturn, Orion,
my head
tore through the clouds,
I bumped my head
on Mars,

the magic starts,
my feet bare,
toes curling
the earth's damp grassblades,

I spell the word
"cancer"
with a
lower case
"c" –

the heavenly bodies
count me:

I am a constellation
made up of stars,
more stars
than any of the gods in the sky
and all of them
bloated
with explosive hope.

6 August 2014
The Doctor,
Part 52

Dark places
attract me,
have always
turned me on,

I go easily,
uncarefully
to dark places
testing,
feeling through
the black ooze,
the lights out,
lone
demonhunter,
monster bait,
inviter of
spirits,

I think I saw
my grandpa Joe
in my bedroom
after he died
when I was four,

he hung over the long window
peacefully,
warm
like a curtain
furling and unfurling
in the blue, after midnight light

and now
there is a
rock python,
(Python sebae),
a son of a bitch

with a particularly
aggressive
reputation
slithering
in my building,

I go easily
to dark places,
I still
hunt them down,
boundaryless,

I am not afraid of
cancer or
snakes

so come,
enter freely and of your own will,
try and take me,

I won't
taste good
sullied with a host of toxins,

I will
stand inside your jaw,
Beowulf rising up,
stretching your bones
'til they crack,
the sharp points
of the broken mandible
piercing and killing
whatever it is
that makes
the dark places
go.

7 August 2014

The Doctor,
Part 53

Every day
I have always
wanted
to impress you,

I am a terrible
dancer
but I have learned
how to pretend
to lead
cause your smile
when I do
is fireworks,

recently, I ripped down
a tower of sad
that was in our way
so we can
march on,
so I can
get back in the ring,
angels
assembling my armor
helmet-to-heart
as I write this,
readying me
to be on top
to be
breathing
like it was easy,
nothing broken,
nothing
cut up
when this next round
is over,
all ready
to ask you
to do a little
bad dancing
with me.

8 August 2014
The Doctor, Part 54

Un peu de peur –
in the bad dreams
I lose parts:

last night I flew to Bern, Switzerland
for an
experimental
procedure,

I got in, I
qualified
for a
promising trial,

Dr. Neil Segal,
Sloan Kettering's
crack ace
met me in the
walk-in freezer,

his cowl
was very
Hazmat,
Otto Preminger
in bell diving gear,

a metal tray between us,
the shiny tools
tucked away,
their tiny shapes
dulled,
undangerous
beneath the blanket,

he told me
in his evereven, evercold way
they were going to
shave my head,
that they would be
shearing off my ears,
my nose,

"that's what we
do here,"
he insisted
on smiling,
his gums clumsy,
unfamiliar
with the act.

11 August 2014
The Doctor, Part 55

It is no great
epiphany that led me
whirling into
some eternal gyre of unique creation,
there is nothing significant or even
benchmark
in it

but it is
a lever
that unlocked
a cog,
that defined
the size and way
of my tools

when, in the fall of
ninety-six or ninety-seven or ninety-eight
as my vision
started to blur
I decided
Book Antiqua,
14-point font,

an imperious cousin
to perfect
Garamond
12-point,

chosen
not for its broad shoulders –
it's overlargeness
bordering on
oafishness –
but because
at an arm's length
away
from my head
I cannot see
12-point poems.

11 August 2014
The Doctor,
Part 56

Ambassador
of life,
I betray my
confidence
in peace
and paint my face
for war,

my allies
the most significant
bonds,
the force
linking the plates of my armor,

my industry
devoted foolishly
through narrow blinders
permits the odd,
empty promise
to eek through,
suctioning
my important flesh,
compromising
everything,

I am painting my face
listening to the sound of the brush
moving across my cheek,
getting ready for war,
checking and paranoid
double-checking
the strength
of my bonds:

don't say
you're going to call
if you're not
going to call.

The Doctor, Part 57

More time I spend at home
the more
I don't like
my neighborhood
very much:

the soul of the thing
is gone,
replaced by quick, safe
housing for the vain,
the privileged,

I am reminded I am in
the wrong place again
bumping into
a true blue
blood,
Peter Davis
from college years –

everyone said,
"kiss hiss ass,
hiss mom's a big
literary agent,"
more recently,
"kiss hiss ass,
hiss mom knows
everyone
at Sloan Kettering "-

I feel the mistake happen
saying hello
like he's
actually a friend,
I can feel
my energy wasted,
the recoil of a bad decision
ascending my arm
like a bad cramp,

Peter takes my hand in his and pushes me away
at the same time
all while seated,
his eyes
up, down, dismissed,
"Nice to see you, Sean,"
he knows I have cancer,
"how are you?
Good to see you, Sean. Okay."
I guess he
doesn't want to talk,

I walk away
slippery with regret
hating all the kind voices,
all that honey
wasted
on an ass-hole.

15 August 2014
The Doctor,
Part 58

Doctor Time,
this is still a very sensitive matter,
time,
but, if you haven't noticed,
I'm heroing up,
holding the reins in my mouth
gritting my teeth
on the leather,
doing the
necessary
roadwork
to adjust the clock
so that the numbers
don't mean so much anymore,

so it's just me
alone with
my cancer,
my
punchingbag,

no one ever warned me
I could be
prey for some
monster,

it was
always
someone else,
someone else's family,
someone else's
husband,

like a snake bite in the woods I never
thought this could happen to me

and now I have it
and it's
winding its way
trying to have me

and it creeps me the fuck out:
FEAR
will make this
impossible,
he's told me as much,
so I sprinkle
little dashes of fear
on my berries
and touch each fruit

like the different
cardinal points
on a
rosary cross
before
efficiently masticating
the smallest, sweetest and most delicious
of anxieties,

I dream, I wake
I don't have cancer
and I feel better
(I still have it),

I put away
the telescope,
the sextant,
I keep my glasses
clean,
I keep them on because
that's
as far
as anyone
needs to see.

17 August 2014
The Doctor,
Part 59

Before I started
with the razor tonight
I was thinking about
staying on the Bay
in Truro
a few weeks ago,
running down
a hundred and ten early morning steps
to the ocean
minutes
before I had to leave
to get a couple of nuggets of time,
a few extra splashes
to heal
just a little bit more,
the tide was low,
covered with unfriendly shells,
pointy rocks,
the water fridge chilly
froze my toes
and
these obstacles,
easy discomfort
had me laughing
alone on the beach
at all the things I've done
recently – all
the treatments,
operations,
infusions –
and how bad
a few sharp shells
and a quick invigorating blast
with such
obvious bliss
a leap into the waves away:

the hair I shaved off my head
tonight
is much uglier
lining the smooth, bright white curves
inside and around
the mouth
of the wide porcelain sink,

the hair seems more
colorless,
foreign,
lifeless
off my head,

is much uglier
scattered all over the
white ceramic floor tiles
which themselves
look dingier
under my old hair,
the white pulled away by wet air,

some hair
fell out,
some hair
stopped growing
as if salted by the Romans,
some,
the most appealing,
appears determined,

I trimmed it all down
to a quarter inch,
the result in the mirror
without
the luxurious disguise,
the sexual distraction offered by
hair

is serious and honest,
gentler and more fierce.

20 August 2014
The Doctor,
Part 60

In my blood
dragon fire:
Aloxi,
Adrocil,
Benadryl,
Fluoracil,
Sodium chloride,
Decadron,
Erbitux,
Wellcovorin,
Zofran,
Compazine,
Atavan,
Xanax,
Lioresal,
Clobetasol (cream),
Clobetasol (shampoo) –

nothing
gold

and it still surprises me
when it makes me
sick,
all this medicine
throttling my system –

the new thing
is now I have acne,
level two
Doctor Ryan said –
a painful plague
on my face, on my nose, in my nostrils,
on my groin and my back

and on my head –
some of the poison, the tumors,
some of the cancer
oozing out,

I have lost hair,
I've lost weight
(I am
one sixty-nine
for the first time
in decades),

messing with my head,
messing with my
Dorian Gray,
messing with
my future,

the quickest glimpse
too far forward
is a tidal wave of drowning sand,
there's more coming down the pike,
there's more
scares the shit out of me:
surgery
and that I hope
for surgery,
maybe
radiation,
maybe
little radioactive microballs
might be placed
inside my liver,

I get weak,
the medicine gets in
and taps
all I have,
shows me pictures
of the
great man
who will
replace me
in my bed,
reading
to my little girl,
I betray
all my work,
I am NOT
easy
on myself,
failed
again,
spineless coward,

the self hatred
works for me
smoothing my cheek
on the canvas
so I remember
what it's like
to be face down
so I remember
I don't like it,
I make it
up again,
do the pushups,
do the diet,
do the
meditation,

I intimately hate you,
my fears,
weak, selfish
shit,

I make it
up again,
strong,
probably
stronger
because
beating you
is what all this is about
and
I can't wait
to get there,
the independence,
the lingering
mine to wolf.

22 August 2014
The Doctor, Part 61

Allover in pimples,
chemically castrated –
radioactively,
the only child
I can have now
at best
a sad nightmare,

rarely am I quiet,
part
Irish Setter,
part
truffle hound
I am unable
to just let
anything
go –

so
forgive me
my savagery
if I keep on
tearing away
at it,
a prisoner
at the desperate
beginnings of
a modest tunnel
out –

a maddening certainty
under all this
pus and poison
there has to be
something true,
some
reason.

23 August 2014
The Doctor,
Part 62

Sick,
being sick,
looking
sick
you need,
irrationally,
more,
an insatiable vacuum,
a love like a scream
with a planetary
gravitational field

and just like
outer space
the loneliness,
the unique isolation of having a disease,
of being
contaminated
stretches
so far
it quiets
everything.

1 September 2014

The Doctor,
Part 63

Indigenous predators
there are
two serpents
slippery as a narrow ledge,

they stalk,
they watch,
I snatch
glimpses
in the shaving mirror
when I apply my
I'm not dying
brave face war paint,

the one
over my left shoulder,
despair,
the one on the right,
hope
cries me to masturbate:

it's going to be okay,

the words,
the words
soothe me,
my onanism,
my kundalini,
my embrace,

I am the only one
every day,
quixotic
to tell myself
everything is going to be okay,
so, please
gather with me
under this perfectly safe canopy of no bullshit:

every time I lay down
on a bed
on a couch
on the grass
the first thing I think of
looking up
is being on an operating table,

I shake all over and stand up,
I get
horny desperate,
wrap my arms
around myself
tight
to get strong,

staring into
the glass
I see
the pain,
the skin getting tighter,
the honesty in being angry
and disappointed,

the toughest son of a bitch ever to dream in my head
daring me,

if I don't look into the mirror
then I can forget I have cancer

but I look
and dream today
you're going
to live.

6 September 2014
The Doctor,
Part 64

I see a podiatrist for the first time on Monday morning.

Maybe I thought I'd
catch the tiger by the toe,
the cancer
by the toe
when I performed
Botched Home Surgery
like me
playing the violin
or
the alto sax,

it started with a thorn
like the story of the Lion and the Mouse,
a thorn of a toenail
burrowing into the
the left side of the large toe on my left foot,

the thorn was about halfway down the toe
and there was
no mouse:

I placed my foot on the flat toilet seat
(I kept the lid
closed
in case I lost
a toe)
and positioned the toenail clippers
at the top of the nail
pointing downward
at an angle
to the left,

the act was a metaphysical experience,
a surreal distraction
from the tumors in my liver,
the one in my colon,
a desperate departure like slicing open an eyeball
to keep me from
feeling the chemo,

maybe this was something I could mouse, I could fix
without a doctor
for once,

I cut down
at an angle
stopping
halfway down
then I turned left
cutting horizontally and
adjusted the toenail clippers
so they were now
miniature pliers
grabbing onto the badger tail of the hidden thorn
I pulled,
tearing this round,
sharp edged fishhook
free from my toe,

bright white
pearls of pus
blooming
where I opened the toe's eye.

6 September 2014
The Doctor,
Part 65

I am an agent
of change,
NASA,
a secret agent
and I want to take
my cancer to space.

8 September 2014
The Doctor, Part 66

If it wins,
my living will:

if there are any questions
ask my wife,
her wisdom is lean and
fiercely abbreviated,

I want a Viking funeral,
to ride a pyre on the currents,
the East River
pulling me
under the City's tremendous bridges
out to sea

but,
even with the questionable debris
and the militant pollutants
that make up
the East River
there would be
expensive obstacles,
mostly legal,
perhaps
some moral

and this should be easy, cheap, alive,

I do not wish to be buried,
I do not wish
absurd expenses to be paid
for a stupid magic show
where what's left of me
winds up stuck in a box
haunting the worms of eternity,

please get rid of the body,
cheap and easy,
burn it,

but first, let's have a pool party
someplace warm,
Malibu, New Mexico, Colorado,
Va'vau, Tonga,
my friends,
my family
surrounding me in a kidney-shaped pool
like a happy ending to
John Cheever's "The Swimmer"

salty kisses to my forehead,
my pink ears,
my thin eyelids
my chlorine nape,
salty kisses
feeding me
painkillers and sweet cocktails,
hands all over
floating me in my favorite Hawaiian shirt
to the deep end
the sun bouncing off the prism ripples,
let me float
to the bottom

and then, yeah, burn me down,
I've done a little research –
there are costs associated with
organ donation,
(you have to pay the doctor
to harvest the organ,

you have to pay the driver
to transport the organ)
and it looks like the medical schools
might give me back
when they're done –
I don't want
my ass to get dragged around
in pieces
only to come home
again some day,
W.W. Jacobs'
monkey's paw,
turning up like so many hot strawberries in a Ziploc bag
so what I want, please, is
burn me down,
put my bones and ashes
in a bell jar,
something clear
so I don't get mixed in
with cookies
or pancakes
the morning
before you toss me in the ocean,
my loves.

11 September 2014
The Doctor,
Part 67

The doctor
warned me
the nausea would be
worse:

I jump up
around 4 or 5
because the devil needs to sing,

my jaw
cranes open
but there's no food,
just clear,

I poke,
reaching with my finger
looking for a hook
a handle to tug
to pull up
the thing that's making me wretch
but I get nothing,
just clear, bubbly mucus
and a sore throat,

the doctor
worries
I'm losing weight,

the doctor
worries
I've lost
fifteen pounds
since July,

I say
Doc,
I don't drink
six beers a night,
I changed my diet
eight weeks ago – I don't eat
bread,
cheese
or sugar
anymore

so if you and your cocktail
stop making me
sick
you can stop worrying,
I can stop puking
and we'll be magic.

12 September 2014
The Doctor, Part 68

Things,
things are not going
the way I had hoped
very quickly:

I trapeze
between
am I near the end
and everything else.

13 September 2014
The Doctor,
Part 69

I don't want to be
the man on the table
anymore,

I want to be
the concerned friend
the tense muscles on my face
gushing love
at my bedside:

I go and go,
it's been
only
three months,

already
three months and the
discomfort,
the discomforts
mount
and spread so there is now
always
something that hurts,
tiny, Count of Monte Cristo
maddening pains,
excessive ingrown nails as my skin
stretches,
the little dry daggers
in the middle of my
sores,
the leper's plague of acne
smeared on my chest, my back,
the most painful,
the most stabbing
on my scalp and

behind my ears
so it hurts
to lay down —

I have trouble believing
it's going to get
better
than this,
than
constant
pain,

I go and I go
carried along
by the momentum of survival,
by a
singular option,

it's been
only
three months
already
and I
hate
I don't want to be
the man on the table
anymore.

16 September 2014
The Doctor, Part 70

I've had the same dream twice,
it makes
my breath tight:

the day is beautiful,
the sky is blue,
the grass is lush summergreen
and I am naked
running the length of a fence made of
linens on the line
drying in the wind,

gathered on the grey, wooden porch
my
most loving friends,
my wife, my daughter,
my mother, my sister,
my
uncle and aunt,
my cousins
all have guns,
some of them are
old, well-oiled,
well loved,
beautiful gunmetal,
some are slicker,
cheaper,
unreliable,

disposable
after doing crimes,
Tess' gun is much too large,
a longass .45,
I notice
the kick
will probably
knock her down
and she is likely
to shoot someone else,
my mother has a big, steel .38 and
my wife is holding a
tactical AK-47 –
hopefully set on single shot,

smoke and fire and ozone
they all start shooting at me -

the shadow behind the sheets,
I move like the devil –

the ones that hit
bite
like
burning angry hot
beestings
under.

25 September 2014
The Doctor, Part 71

As you predicted,

I look different,
not gaunt yet,
not different enough
to be resentful
yet,

my hair
has been
salted by the Romans,
I am
covered
with scales,

I can dress up
to make
you
feel better,

maybe
I don't look as good,
anyway, baby,

but if you want to come by
I picked up
those mushrooms
you wanted
to get for your girl and you.

25 September 2014
The Doctor,
Part 72

For eight weeks –

eight
fucking
weeks
of poison

then
after stripping you
down,
dressing you
in an ill fitting, ugly-striped
gown
and putting you in
a very cold room
to wait
long enough
to get really scared,

they put you in a tube
to see
if the poison's working

"Okay. Put your arms over your head.
Breathe.
Breathe in.

Hold it."
then they make you wait,
seemingly reasonable
people,
other
humans
make you
beg
for the precious,
am I going to die this week?!
precious
RESULTS

and this greedy waiting
whispering what if
over and over
is
the worst poison
with
the worst
side effects.

25 September 2014
The Doctor,
Part 73

There are
tiny wounds,
open sores
that wait
too long
to heal,

there is
no feeling
sometimes
in my fingertips,

the other day
my whole hand
froze,
went numb
feeling through the keys,
falling
like a drunk
against the doorknob.

25 September 2014
The Doctor, Part 74

Floating,
I float,

I am learning
a fear
of hospitals,
doctors,
that ilk,

when it gets quiet as concrete
under those lights
take my hand
so I don't
float away.

27 September 2014
The Doctor, Part 75

Standing at an angle
to the left of the toilet
the round bulbs in the bathroom
aren't very bright
but in the mirror beneath the lights
I can see
my three quarter profile
and
this is the first time I've seen my skeleton –

hair gone,
fat gone,
cheeks, the features all accented
by the
pointy edges of my bones
poking beneath the skin,
sharper

and,
stained clam-tail grey with some
dark chemo spots
dotting the tip,
a dangling, characterless ribbon
it may as well be
another line,
another plastic IV
for nothing more than pissing toxins
out of me.

27 September 2014
The Doctor,
Part 76 (for Kiki)

So, Kiki,
you and me,
we'll hang out
in this
hospital room
together

sneaking around
in our
civilian clothes
and not those
vulnerable,
icky
patient's robes
even though
we're patients

and we'll pry the door open
just enough
to prop a bucket on top

then,
in a high-pitched,
Graham Chapman-in-drag voice,
we say something like,
"oh, hey, Cancer,
you forgot your piece of
coffee cake in here,
you silly"

and when
the Ass-hole
comes through the door,
the bucket falls and
Our Cancer
gets covered with
molecular acid

and then,
you and me,
we LAUGH
like Christmas.

ISE TO

ISE TO

SE TO

SE TO

To do *Everything* so your
the *Hospital* and doesn't come *Back.*

28 September 2014
The Doctor,
Part 77

Dear Tess,
I promise
to do
everything
so your father
never
goes to the hospital
and
doesn't come back.

1 October 2014

The Doctor,
Part 78

After the doctor told me
no more chemo,
I knew it when she said it
but it's time
for
next steps,
time to put on
a peppermint-striped pair of long johns
and jump
feet first
into the unknown
again,

I came home
a little elated,
no more chemo
for now,

shit, I might
lose the scales,
grow back some hair,
get back some fat,
feel fucking good
for a few weeks,

then the snake
thick as a potato,
the
largest tumor,
inflamed, hard,
resting
to the right of my belly button
shifts,
creeping me the fuck out,
reminding me

time to think
about having a
surgical steel
hockey puck
stuck
under my ribs,
some tube
sticking out of my side
maybe forever
so I have a longer,
weirder
life –

I don't want to die,
I can't die
yet
but can I live
like a wind-up clock,
a radioactive
cyborg?,
what does comfort
look like
then
for me,
for the people in my life? –

my father's copy of "John Brown's Body"
was falling apart
so I placed it
and a book about Gramercy Park by Carole Klein
on top of the trash bins
thinking
some nostalgian,
someone who likes to noodle around in words from the past
might pick them up,

this morning around four I got sick,
working the remaining chemo
out,
showered,
delicately washed
my scales,
dressed
and sat outside
on my black diamond-plate stoop
to smoke the ease into me,
to relax the spasms,
to hot cocktail the dread,
to caterpillar blue smoke around my head,
who are YOU?
and the leaves on the ground
turn quickly over
to Brown pages
filled with small, old,
somewhat erotic type,

the loose pages
of my father's book
all the way down the sidewalk and the street,
chilly,
urban
autumn
laid out
waiting for the lasers to start humming.

1 October 2014

The Doctor,
Part 79

160 pounds of
angry,
160 pounds
of love,
160 pounds
of Sean,
I cry out,
I beg
please stop
to an empty room,
feeling and feeling
this Thing
and today
it feels
like I'm losing,

I have never
had to be
a hero
in a nightmare,

to be
super,

to fight
my very hardest

while a monster
tries to kill me.

8 October 2014
The Doctor,
Part 80

Contemplating my dream,
feeling up and down
on my right side
where the tumors
are swollen:

a week of nothing,
a week of
no pain,
of comfort,
no doctors,
my wife and I smiling,

and the friends
who get me there
flood my eyes –

sure,
there have been
promises of food, of soup, of drives
that never appear
but sometimes
the desperate love
behind the
start of the gesture
is enough
and struggling with mortality
fills you with the oddest
forgiveness
when people remember
to apologize –

even the bully from high-school
who slammed me into the locker
for giving his girl
a copy of Borges'
The Book of Imaginary Beings
has been tender,

all the people
from Bennington College
I thought I'd pissed off
forever
surprise me
by being there.

And then,
after denouncing
the pharmaceuticals
and announcing
the comfort,
the EUREKA! relief
in the pain
of my liver tumors
by taking concentrated doses of THC
that are extremely
tricky
to procure,
soon,
slick as a weasel
in among all this
like the creepiest junkie rat
an old college classmate wrote me
in shitbag English:

Yo Sean! Been following along on here.
Sorry you're having to go thru dis shit.
I was interested in $ome of your throw away meds.
I love Vikes but can't get it or anything along those lines.
Also would love to try a gold cap.
They look awesome.

I told him to try and get some cancer
so the
world could be
his oyster.

10 October 2014
The Doctor,
Part 81

The people in the other room –
my family –
the people
I see on the street
all look different,

there is no
anti-AIDS like
campaign
against
victims of cancer

but The Healthy Ones can tell
I am changing
and the fear spreads
out from the base of operations
inside
to the
Halloween costume
I am wearing,

there's a lot of
hands off,
the long blue-green hallway of my next hospital visit
the way my sleep
starts lately:

gurney smooth,
craning my neck
against the meds.

10 October 2014
The Doctor,
Part 82

When I wake
I tell my wife
I love her
like it's the first time,

when I get outside
my father is already
flying,

he says,
don't get too close, Sean,
this stuff
can burn you real bad,

I lie to my father
and move closer.

10 October 2014
The Doctor,
Part 83

The hurt feels homeless,

I don't know
where to go
to make it stop,

my doctor
doesn't return
my call,

I don't want
another
waiting room,

I'm ready
to crawl
under the porch

find some
cold dirt.

12 October 2014
The Doctor,
Part 84

Several months ago,
maybe after the
first eight weeks of chemo had ended
and before the
next eight weeks of chemo started,
my practical wife,
I think it was
Cecilia
speaking for us
who asked
The Doctor
what it would be like
to die
of liver failure,
in case the tumors just
keep growing
because they just
keep growing,

The Doctor said it wouldn't be
terribly painful,
(except maybe THIS part?)
there would be
some
overall bloating
and
I would eventually
fall asleep,

so I worry,
not sleeping
about being overly tired
and I worry
when my belly
looks
abnormally
round,

I haunt the walls
with my groans
sliding like
a flying Dutchman,
doomed to travel between
whatever
circle-steady hell of pain I am
and my medicines,
driven mad
as fewer of them
succeed
in helping:

it is difficult for me
to sit still,
I can tell
something is wrong,
something the size of my
fist
and I panic,
I begin
to let go to the things that make me happy,

unloading

so I can still fight

without being weighed down

by the steady management

of pain,

by my penis doesn't work,

by I don't really sleep,

by I am still in real goddamn shock,

by the shock you into your bones fear that doesn't go away

from the

initial

diagnosis

in May

and I've gone from

The Doctor pointing at my liver in the spring

to October,

my liver

pointing at me,

challenging me

to remain

on

my feet,

to

strengthen up

for the

next procedures,

the

next day

in the hospital

three days from now.

13 October 2014
The Doctor,
Part 85

A perfect evening:
the air was tender!

It was our first night
alone together
in months,

over dinner
our words were soft,
the way our mouths moved
when we talked,
when we moved
alone together,

The Doctor walked into the bedroom,
a fresh coffee stain
around the button where her lapels meet,
I was surprised
she didn't knock
until
The Doctor struck her,
open handed
and the devil in me
came out,
might as well have hit her too,
she cried
alone in the bathroom.

14 October
2014

THE Doctor, PART 86 I HATE THIS POETRY: Su
A Good LIFE and I got a piece of the DEVIL
I wish I WAS TOUGH, I wish I could pour a tough to
I Got Before the storm picks up an

ood like so so Lucky, Such,
Me getting bigger like a Storm,
Drink over the HOT Fear
s to carry Me Away

14 October 2014
The Doctor,
Part 86

I hate this poetry:

such a good life,
so, so
lucky,
such
a good life
and I got a piece of the devil inside me

getting bigger
like a storm,
angrier
like a dog tied to a tree
during the storm,

I wish I was a tough,
I wish
I could pour
a tough guy's drink
over
the hot fear I got

before the storm
picks up
and tries
to carry me away.

22 October 2014
The Doctor, Part 87

Swirling waters,
I have seen
the meanest me
under
this cancer moon,

rabid tornado,
cornered, snapping
savage
turning
on my love and my love and my nurse and my friend –

after I
turn back
naked quick
I measure,
I weigh
the nightmare,
squeeze the juice
out of judgment
trying to
get it perfect,
to be my greatest –

I am bigger, above,
my love
is better than that.

16 October 2014

The Doctor,
Part 88

"I never saw a wild thing
sorry for itself."
— *D.H. Lawrence*

Between
the very high floor
and the very
low ceiling
I pace the cage
purring my cheek
against the firm corners,
desperate
for affection,
preparing for violence,

decorative bruises,
tiger stripes
ring the shaft of my cock,
my right testicle
is warrior purple
after six hours of surgery
exactly one week ago

and tomorrow
I'm jumping through
the flaming hoop,

I'm jumping in
for them to
strap me down again
in one day,

one day
to get ready
for more
pain –
radioactive
pain
for I'm not sure how long,

to get ready
for more deep bruising,
more tiger,
wild
I need to be held
I can't be held,
I can
walk tight, low circles
in a cage.

22 October 2014
The Doctor,
Part 89

Riding an ever shifting current of discomfort
I try to stay safely in the middle of the boat,

I try to distract myself by
looking at beautiful things,
by watching beautiful things,
trying to touch
beautiful things,

I kneel down and lap at them
at the risk of falling in,
of looking ridiculous
before I disappear,

all my thirst,
all my reflection.

27 October 2014
The Doctor, Part 90

Near the end of October
the yellowest light
pours down
during the day,
at least 'til three,
and seems to shine
just as bright during the night,

I stand
in that light
misshapen
in our apartment window and
lift my shirt
to take account,
to look
to smooth my hand
over the tumors
where they grow
round my abdomen,
left side
and right,
I pretend that I can try and see
the radioactivity,
the teeny, tiny microspheres
the doctor
put inside my liver Thursday,

I talk to my body,
look over my shoulder
watching out for
mistakes
and was that a wrong turn?,
the conversation we have is like steering
a river narrowing
on both sides,
afraid
the wheel
might have
only two,
maybe three turns
left in it,

this close
to the end of the year,
it feels like
it should be the end of something.

1 November 2014
The Doctor,
Part 91

Talking movies,
horror movies
with my buddy Dan
in the kitchen,
The Omen,
he grabs it in his meaty fist,
he declares
the original is the best,
I watched myself sedate my debate –
and it's not all untrue –
but when he told me
as a child he walked by
that church,
All Saints Church in Fulham, London SW6,
the frame of the window behind him became bigger
and more light came in,
I wasn't thinking
about movies anymore,
I was happy with my childhood
and compared it
to walking by that church
going and coming that way
for school,
my own sudden monuments
creepy, leering, filled with the unknown
that I quietly walked
past
through my safe, rabbit-like, bully-free
paths
from home to school and back
as dark and beautiful
but I was glad to feel envious,
I embraced the envy of
walking under such a foreboding edifice.

2 NOVEMBER 2014   THE Doctor, PART 92

Dear Doctor,

Please
tell me you were wrong
SIX MONTHS AGO,
THAT it's not
CANCER,
THAT it WAS Just
A SMEAR of bird SHit
ON a computer screen
A Smudge on the SCAN.

dear Docter,

I AM EXHAUSTED,

ASS up. FACE DOWN on the CANVAS.
HUMiliATED
by the boot on MY NECK,
so close
to broken
I CAUGHT MYSELF
CRYING WITH A GARBAGE bag in   MY HAND
ON SUNDAY,

dear Doctor, I AM SO AFRAID   I SHAKE. SO SCARED I'll NEV
or see the SNOW SWALLOW THE EARTH   SO TELL ME, PLEASE, IT'S J

2 November 2014

The Doctor,
Part 92

Dear Doctor,
please
tell me you were wrong
six months ago,
that it's not
cancer,
that it was just
a smear of bird shit
on the computer screen,
a smudge on the scan,

dear Doctor,
I am exhausted,
ass up, face down on the canvas,
humiliated
by the boot on my neck,
so close
to broken
I caught myself
crying with a garbage bag in my hand on Sunday,

dear Doctor,
I am so afraid
I shake,
so scared
I'll never take the garbage out again
or see the snow
swallow the earth
so tell me,
please,
it's just gas,
it's just
a wrong scallop,
some bad
takeout,
anything
but death.

10 November 2014
The Doctor,
Part 93

Echoes of everything I have taught myself
race around my brain
whining like two-stroke motorcycles in a round cage,

I have to be
at the hospital
for surgery
at seven this morning,

I get up at two-thirty after a solid six,
I am Jackie Gleason
as Fats
in "The Hustler":

I clean up good, snip my
nails,
shave,
there's even a bath with bubbles
where I blow smoke,
my concerns move out over the clear spots in the water
and all the way down to the drain,
swirling away through the pipes with the soap,

I am left naked,
I judge what's left,
I meditate,
stretch,
I
press up against the earth,
every moment past three a countdown
and, as it gets closer,
as the hospital,
as the knife
gets closer
the countdown turns into a drag-strip christmas tree,
the thunder of the racers
champing the bit,
the lights shooting from red to green –

SEVEN!!

that's when the ozone,
the engine,
the air
are gone –
I hear nothing but the quiet of my own calm,

I am
a happy warrior
ready to be
stabbed, shaved, sliced, probed,
poked and scanned.

13 November 2014
The Doctor, Part 94

The bathtub has always been my favorite place,
my Walden Pond, my
Lazarus Pit, my
dream soup –

it is the first place the child in my mind thinks to hide when it's time for me
to go to the hospital again –

always
just hot enough that
when my
gluteus maximus
rests upon the bottom of the ocean floor
and the warm water
envelops my kundalini
I check
left to right,
floor tile to floor tile
to see if there are any
witnesses,
even a passing
water bug,
a silverfish
to testify
that I was comfortable,
that I consumed
a rare,
transforming moment of transport,
a human sigh
luxuriating in the simple pleasure of hot water:

I trust my head
back
just so my ears
break the thin surface,
I can hear my heartbeat,
I try calling
dead people I love with the rotary phone in my mind
to ask
if they think I'm doing okay,
if I'm making
the right decisions,
if they
know anything –

it's still, the noise
a static swell
under the water –

looking up
reminds me of surgery
again,

I breathe away the panic,
I breathe
all the calm out of the
lavender in the soap,
raise my head
slowly like it was in someone else's hands,
above the waterline,

the tub is still
hot enough,
I look around and check,
I'm okay,
I'm doing
okay
and, because it's almost new,
because I
don't know
how long I
get this
this time
and
because it's like hiding
I feel guilty for feeling good.

23 November 2014
The Doctor,
Part 95

Usually
just as I
give up, give
myself,
offering my loyalty
to the
exhaustion,
to the sleep,

it has all the flavor
of PTSD –

each panic
strikes fast, it begins with
what feels like a last gasp,
my face pressed against the wrong side of
the coffin lid

last Tuesday following surgery
they ran me through the narrow tunnel of the petscan,
drugged,

the drugs wore off and I attacked the machine,
smashing the cheap plastic with the bottom of my fist
announcing to the technicians
this is enough,
I'm done,
I don't care if it's
only
another four minutes,

the nurse asked me to stop cursing
like it was a muscle I was flexing for show,
they wouldn't let me out,
they couldn't,
they said I would have to
start over,
another 45 minutes,

they called the doctor and the doctor
gave me more drugs,
sedating my intense claustrophobia,
allowing me to safely
shut my eyes
for four more minutes

only for it to come back
every night,
every time I close my eyes
a rush like a giant wave of unreasonable
smothers me with terror,
sends me
running for the lights,
for the windows,
seeking something I can trust:
some air, some light.

6 December 2014
The Doctor,
Part 96

There's a hell in my head
and I can't get away:

cry, cry, cry,
let's kiss
salty
through the cancer,
past
the tears, let's
collapse
together
like long sighs
and keep busy,
busy enough to forget about it,
at least
how bad it is,
playing Scrabble
or Monopoly in bed,
working circles
around our kid's Christmas list,
going over the same cook books
we have
like there's
going to be
some
surprise
on our menu
this year.

17 December 2014
The Doctor,
Part 97

The way my fingers fit
beginning at the sternum,
moving along
the rib bones,

each time I see
the Doctor,
each time I leave her office
it seems
easier
to say
"I am dying",

I asked again
to grab reality by the tail,
"what if I stop taking
all this medicine,
what if I
stop
doing
all this stuff
that makes me hurt,
that makes me
always
uncomfortable?"

she says she's not sure
but
the studies show
a life expectancy of
six months
without treatment,

I reach
for
the bones in my back
when I scratch them
when I ask
feel like seashells
like an ancient trigger
to
let the water
pour out my eyes,
to
let myself hear it:

"I am dying."

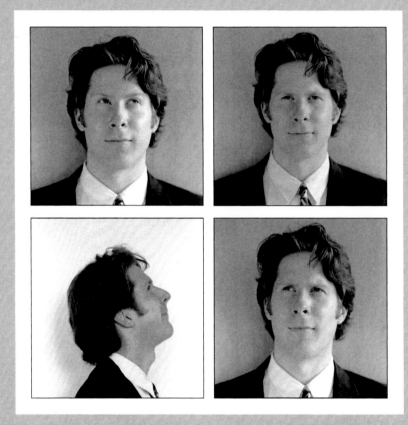

Photo by Dirk Westphal

Brooklyn-based poet, Sean M. Flaherty was born in Stamford, Connecticut on November 15, 1966. He attended Bennington College, Class of 1988, where he studied with Georges Guy and Stephen Sandy. Sean performed his works in various venues in New York, Chicago, and Vermont. Over the course of his writing career, he produced many self-published collections, often collaborating with visual artists and other writers. His work also appeared in a number of literary journals, and in 1994 he was a writer in residence at Ragdale Foundation, an artists' community in Lake Forest, IL. Sean was a huge fan of comic books, video games, and horror movies. He was also an avid soccer fan and an excellent player.

In his professional life, Sean served as Lead Analyst at Rockstar Games in Manhattan, providing quality assurance for the firm's games, including those in the "Grand Theft Auto" series and award winning "LA Noire." Earlier in his career, Sean worked for the Metropolitan Museum of Art and the National Arts Club. He is survived by his wife, Cecilia, daughter, Tess, mother, Kathryn Jackson, and sister, Gordon Jackson.

This book would not have been possible without the immense support and generosity of Rockstar Games and their determination to publish Sean's work. The illustrations accompanying this collection were done by Ciaran Parr.